DEADLIEST ANIMALS

BOX JELLYFISH

BY CONNOR STRATTON

WWW.APEXEDITIONS.COM

Apex is distributed by North Star Editions:
sales@northstareditions.com | 888-417-0195

Produced for Apex by Red Line Editorial.

Photographs ©: iStockphoto, cover; Shutterstock Images 1, 4–5, 6–7, 9, 10–11, 12–13, 14–15, 18–19, 20–21, 22–23, 24–25, 26 (circle), 26 (full page); Jurgen Freund/NaturePL/Science Source, 8; Rubén Duro/Science Source, 15; ANT Photo Library/Science Source, 16–17, 29

Library of Congress Control Number: 2022901425

ISBN
978-1-63738-281-3 (hardcover)
978-1-63738-317-9 (paperback)
978-1-63738-388-9 (ebook pdf)
978-1-63738-353-7 (hosted ebook)

Printed in the United States of America
Mankato, MN
082022

NOTE TO PARENTS AND EDUCATORS

Apex books are designed to build literacy skills in striving readers. Exciting, high-interest content attracts and holds readers' attention. The text is carefully leveled to allow students to achieve success quickly. Additional features, such as bolded glossary words for difficult terms, help build comprehension.

TABLE OF CONTENTS

CHAPTER 1

POISON DARTS

A box jellyfish floats in the ocean water. Shrimp swim nearby. The jellyfish moves toward them.

To move, a box jellyfish pulls water into its body. Then it squirts the water out.

A jellyfish's tentacles shoot darts when something touches them.

The jellyfish's **tentacles** trap the shrimp. Then tiny darts shoot from the tentacles. The darts are filled with **venom**. They hit the shrimp.

DEADLY JELLY

The Australian box jellyfish is the most venomous animal in the ocean. It has killed at least 77 people. However, most box jellyfish can't hurt humans. Only a few kinds can.

FAST FACT

One Australian box jellyfish has enough venom to kill 60 adult humans.

A jellyfish's tentacles can still release poison after the jellyfish dies.

The jellyfish's venom kills the shrimp. The jellyfish uses its tentacles to bring the shrimp to its mouth. Then it eats.

Australian box jellyfish are sometimes called "sea wasps" because of their sting.

CHAPTER 2

LIFE IN THE WILD

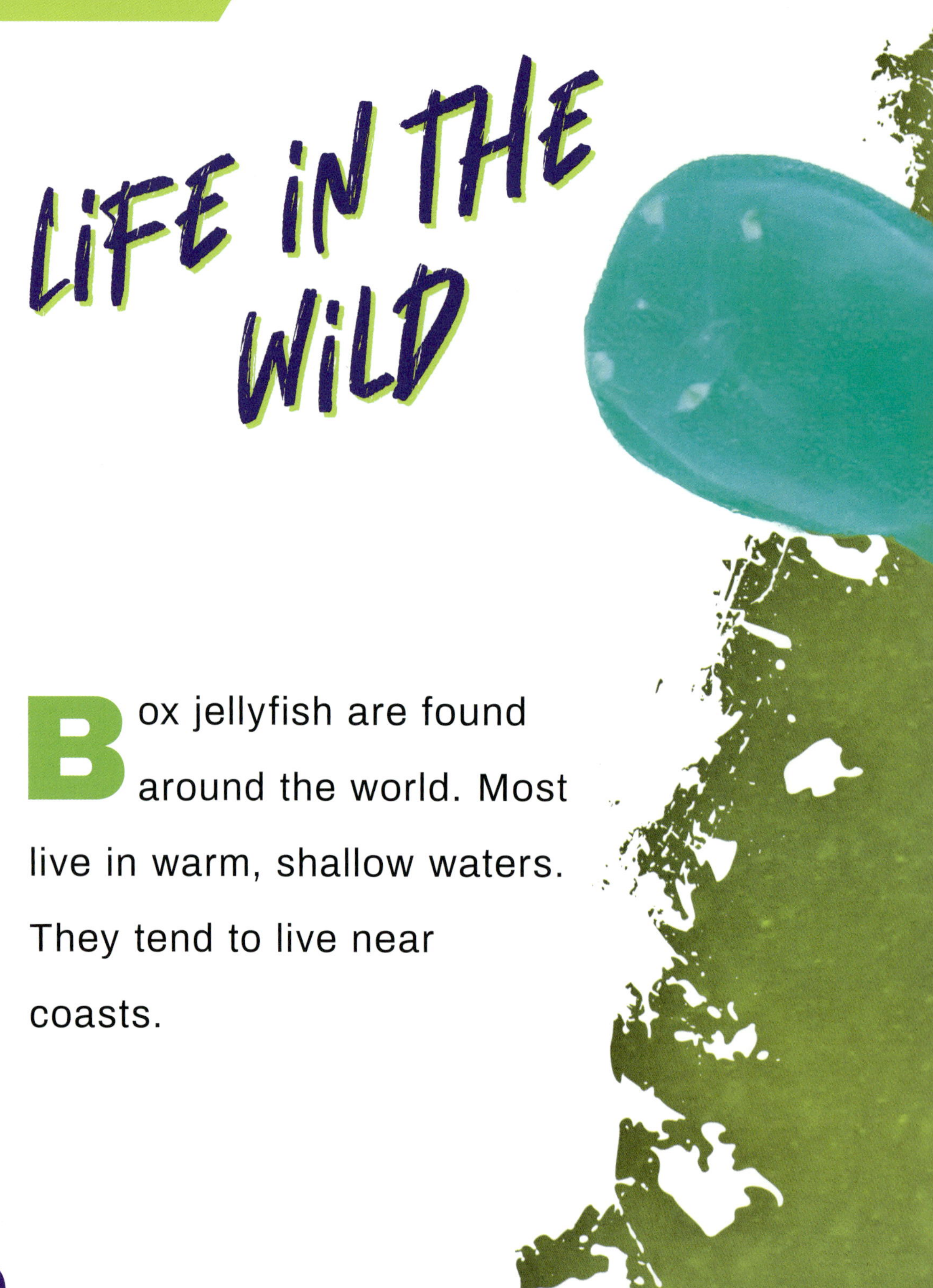

Box jellyfish are found around the world. Most live in warm, shallow waters. They tend to live near coasts.

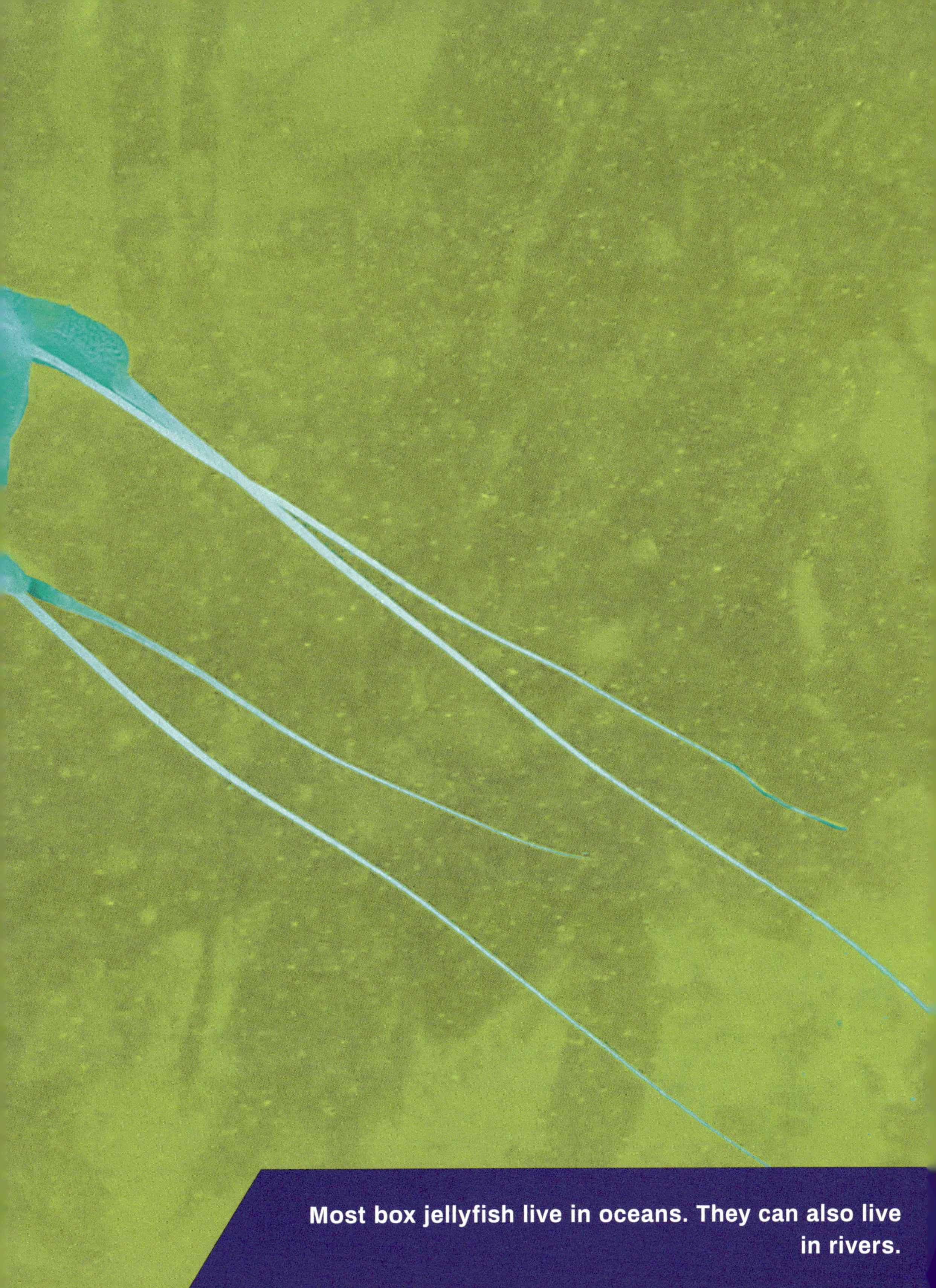

Most box jellyfish live in oceans. They can also live in rivers.

FAST FACT

Some box jellyfish live near mangroves. These trees have many thick roots. They grow along coasts.

Some box jellyfish live in the Atlantic Ocean. But many box jellyfish are found in the Indian and Pacific Oceans. Lots live along Australian coasts.

The roots of mangrove trees provide homes and hiding places for many animals.

Huge groups of jellyfish are called blooms. This photo shows a bloom of moon jellies.

Box jellyfish often live alone. Many come together only when they mate, or have babies. But sometimes, huge numbers of box jellyfish are found together.

A jellyfish life cycle has several stages. The polyp stage looks like a plant.

RIVER MATES

Adult box jellyfish mainly live in salty ocean water. But they also swim to freshwater rivers. They mate there. New jellyfish become adults. They follow the rivers back out to sea.

CHAPTER 3

SOFT BODIES

There are about 50 **species** of box jellyfish. Box jellyfish can have more than 40 tentacles. Some tentacles can grow 10 feet (3 m) long.

Box jellyfish are often see-through or pale blue.

A box jellyfish's body is called a bell. It looks similar to a cube. It has four sides.

FAST FACT

A box jellyfish's bell can be as big as a baseball or as small as a grape.

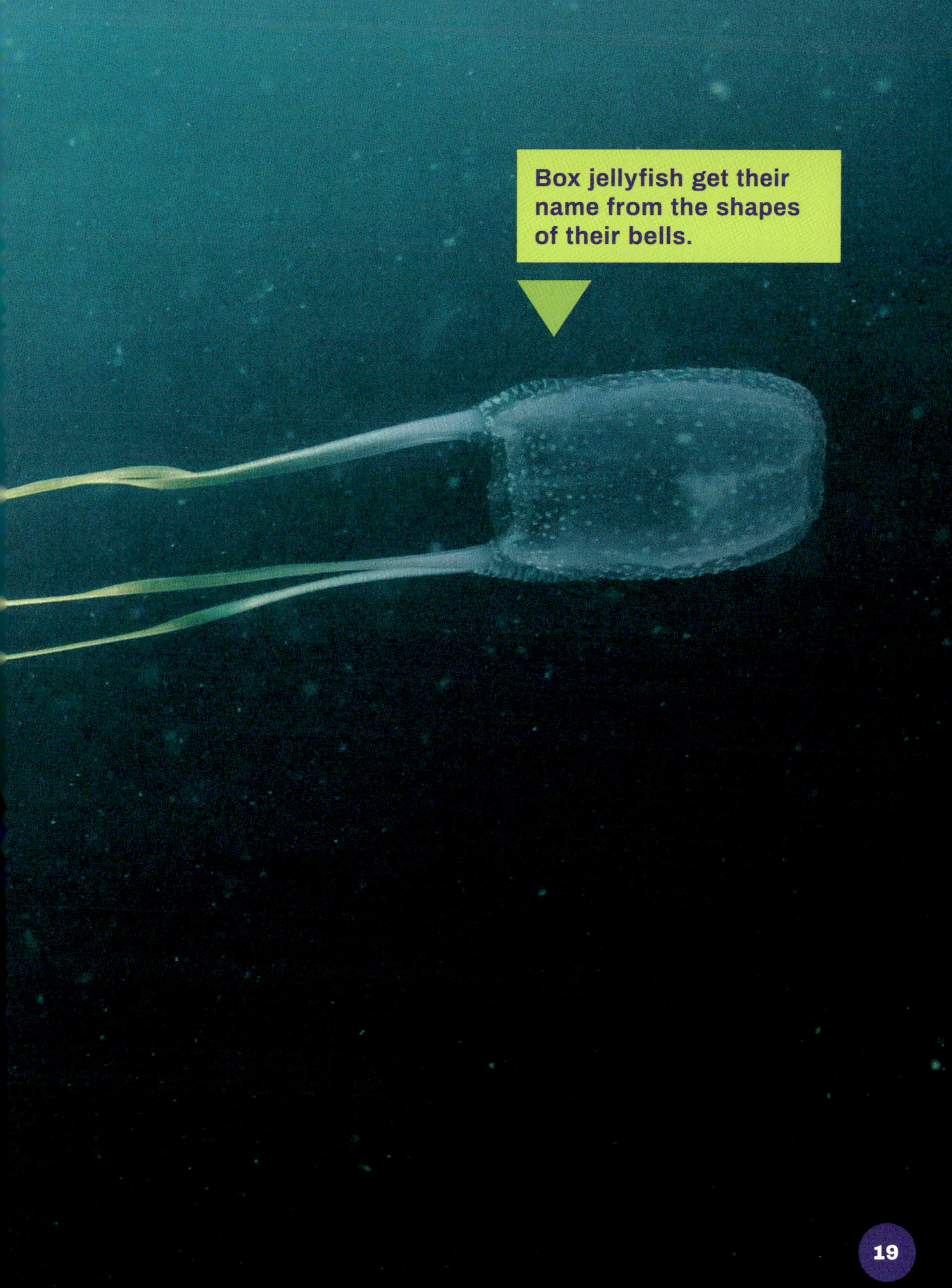
Box jellyfish get their name from the shapes of their bells.

On each side, the jellyfish has a group of eyes. Jellyfish do not have brains. So, scientists don't know how jellyfish understand what they see.

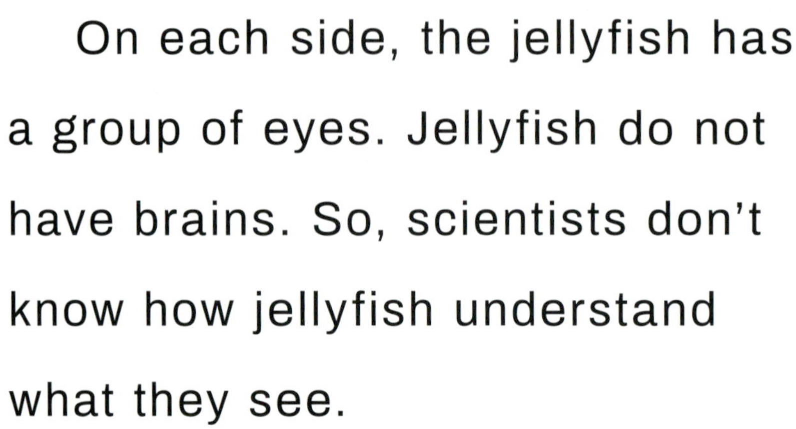

ALL KINDS OF EYES

A box jellyfish has 24 eyes. It has four different types of eyes. Some types are very simple. Others have lenses, like human eyes do.

A jellyfish's groups of eyes look like black dots.

CHAPTER 4

Box jellyfish tend to eat small fish and shrimp. Some eat even smaller things. For instance, a few box jellyfish eat **plankton**.

Box jellyfish are carnivores. They catch and eat other animals.

The lion's mane jellyfish can float long distances in ocean currents.

Most jellyfish mainly float in the water. But box jellyfish move quickly. They can change direction, too. This helps them hunt.

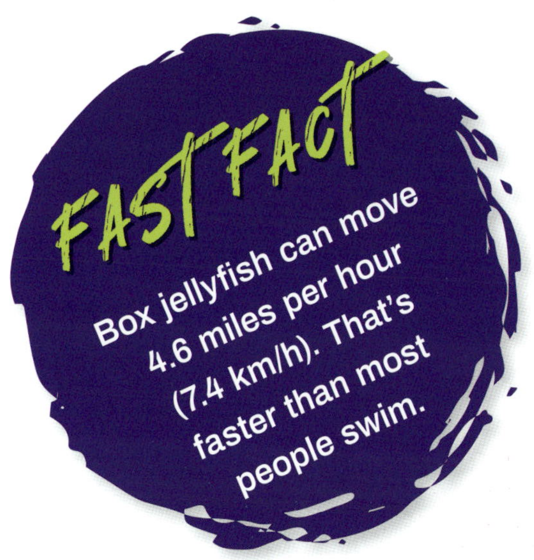

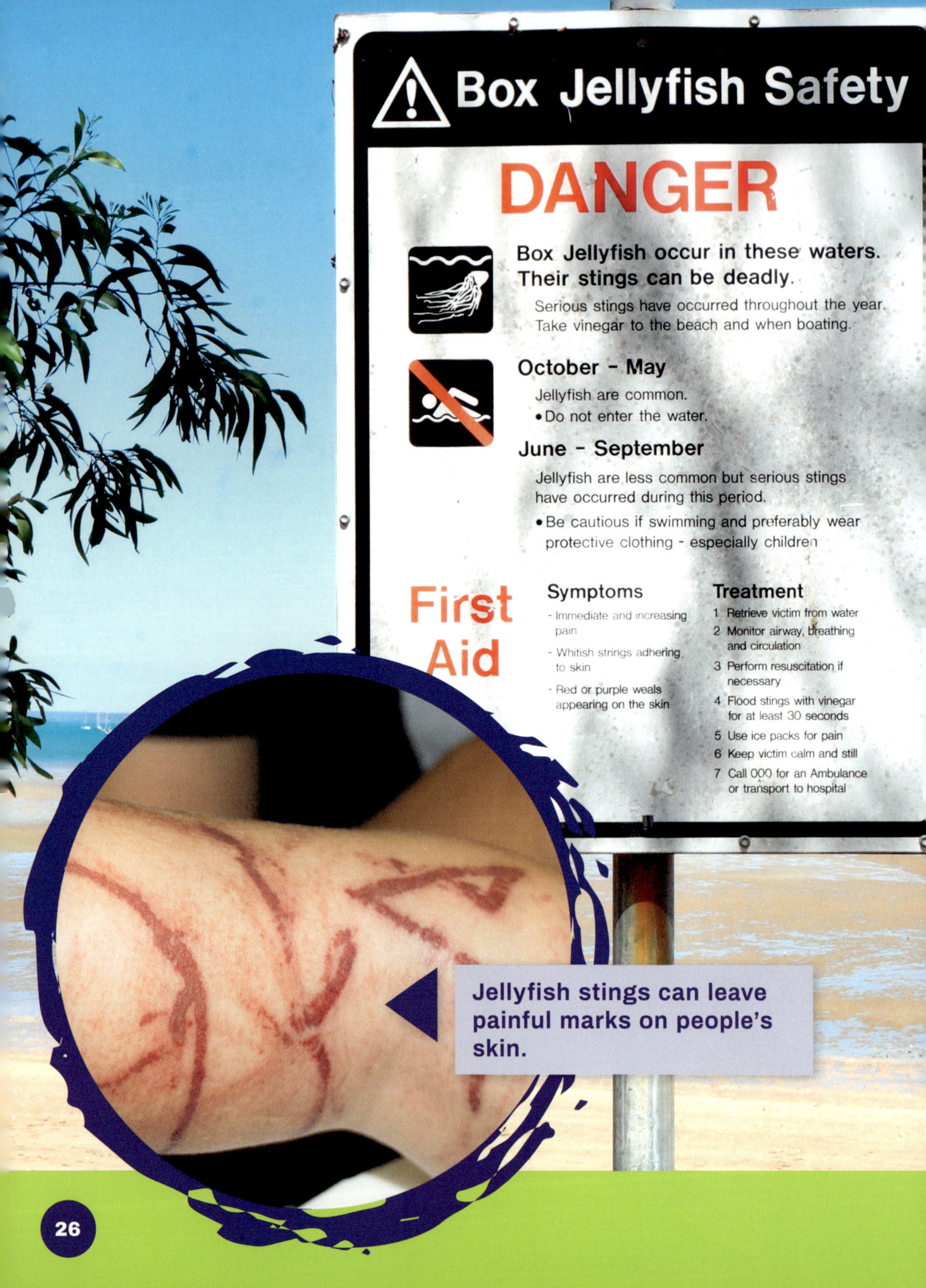

Jellyfish stings can leave painful marks on people's skin.

STRONG STINGS

Box jellyfish can hurt people badly. Their stings are painful. Their poison attacks the heart. It also harms the nerves. Some people get heart attacks. Others still feel pain weeks later.

Box jellyfish venom acts fast. It **stuns** or kills **prey** instantly. The prey cannot move. This helps keep the jellyfish's tentacles safe.

◄ Some beaches use signs to warn swimmers about box jellyfish.

COMPREHENSION QUESTIONS

Write your answers on a separate piece of paper.

1. Write a sentence describing how box jellyfish hunt their prey.

2. Would you want to see a box jellyfish in real life? Why or why not?

3. Which part of a box jellyfish's body holds its venom?

- **A.** its bell
- **B.** its eyes
- **C.** its tentacles

4. How could making prey unable to move keep a box jellyfish's tentacles safe?

- **A.** The prey won't be able to see the tentacles.
- **B.** The prey won't get stung by the tentacles.
- **C.** The prey won't hurt the tentacles by trying to get away.

5. What does **freshwater** mean in this book?

Adult box jellyfish mainly live in salty ocean water. But they also swim to freshwater rivers.

- **A.** water that is salty, like the ocean
- **B.** water that is not salty
- **C.** water that flows through pipes

6. What does **instantly** mean in this book?

Box jellyfish venom acts fast. It stuns or kills prey instantly.

- **A.** after a long time
- **B.** with a loud noise
- **C.** right away

Answer key on page 32.

GLOSSARY

lenses

Curved parts of eyes that help take in light.

nerves

Long, thin fibers that carry information between the brain and other parts of the body.

plankton

Tiny creatures that often float in big groups in the ocean.

prey

An animal that is hunted and eaten by another animal.

species

Groups of animals or plants that are similar and can breed with one another.

stuns

Makes dizzy or unable to move.

tentacles

The flexible limbs of animals such as squid or jellyfish.

venom

A poison made by an animal and used to bite or sting prey.

BOOKS

Clarke, Ginjer L. *Jellyfish!* New York: Penguin, 2021.

Harvey, Derek. *Nature's Deadliest Creatures.* London: DK Children, 2018.

Mattern, Joanne. *Strange Bodies*. South Egremont, MA: Red Chair Press, 2019.

ONLINE RESOURCES

Visit **www.apexeditions.com** to find links and resources related to this title.

ABOUT THE AUTHOR

Connor Stratton writes and edits nonfiction children's books. He is grateful to have never encountered any of the world's deadliest animals.

INDEX

ANSWER KEY:
1. Answers will vary; 2. Answers will vary; 3. C; 4. C; 5. B; 6. C